# Kundalini

# Tarot Guide

Adana Washington

Kundalini Tarot Guide
Copyright: Adana Washington
Published: 23 November 2013
Publisher: The Sassy Tarot Collective

Find out more about the author and upcoming books online at www.adanawtn.com or on Twitter (@adanawtn).

# TABLE OF CONTENTS

# TAROT NUMEROLOGY

## One

Ones are seeds new beginnings. The start of something fresh and clean. They may be a spark of inspiration, an impulsive decision, or the start of a new project.

## Two

Twos are about balance, decisions, and relationships. The are about two halves of a whole, and finding the middle ground between them.

## Three

Threes are the creation. They are the result of collaboration, inspiration, and the decisions that you've made. They are what comes of being ones and two together.

## Four

Fours stand for achievement and stability. You've done the initial work, and you've reaped the first wave of rewards. They signify a time to rest and reflect on your accomplishments before you start working again.

## Five

Fives signify change. It could be a change in status, a change of heart, or the finetuning of things. That change could bring conflict and a bit of misery, but it can also bring hope.

## Six

Sixes are the cards of success, satisfaction and reward. They signal of time of benefits and a chance to relax and revel in the moment.

## Seven

Sevens call for patience, trust and commitment. They represent those times when it's best to be transparent and think about the long term rather than instant gratification.

## Eight

Eights are about progress and priorities. They stand for moving forward in a controlled, structured way. They are the cards that ask you to look at the steps that need to be taken.

## Nine

Nines signal a time of clarity and culmination. These are usually the times when you see the end and know what you have to do to get there  either because it's so close, or because you've already made it.

## Ten

Tens are the completion of the cycle. They stand for the finish line, where lessons are learned and rewards or consequences are reaped. They make the end of one journey and the beginning of another.

## Court Card

Court cards are generally people in your life, or aspects of yourself that you either have been putting forth, or need to bring out into the open. Sometime, they can signify a certain type of situation as well. Either way, when tallying up the theme of the reading, I count Court Cards as follows:

- **Pages** = Ones (Messages, new beginnings, young folk)

- **Knights** = Twos (Decisions, balance, movement)

- **Queens** = Threes (Creativity, feminine energy, fertility)

- **Kings** = Four (Stability, masculine energy, authority)

# MAJOR ARCANA

The Trumps are the archetypes that represent major life themes and changes. They represent those times that you actually remember years from now, not the everyday mundane.

FOOL

# THE FOOL

It's the start of a brand new journey. Pack your shit and hit the road. No need to question your path, or any potential dangers. This is a time when none of that matters  all that matters is that you start moving forward. Just be sure not to do anything exceedingly stupid.

**Key Phrase:** Follow Your Bliss
**Astrological Correspondence:** Uranus

**What's Happening:**
- A new relationship
- A new job or class
- A chance to take a vacation or follow some crazy dream
- Being childish or stupid

**What To Do:**
- Throw caution to the wind
- Get excited
- Go after an opportunity with enthusiasm
- Stop doubting yourself
- Think about the consequences

**Questions to Ask Yourself:**
1. What does this new adventure look like?
2. What do I need to let go of in order to move forward?
3. How can I avoid looking foolish?
4. What leap of faith would I have to take?

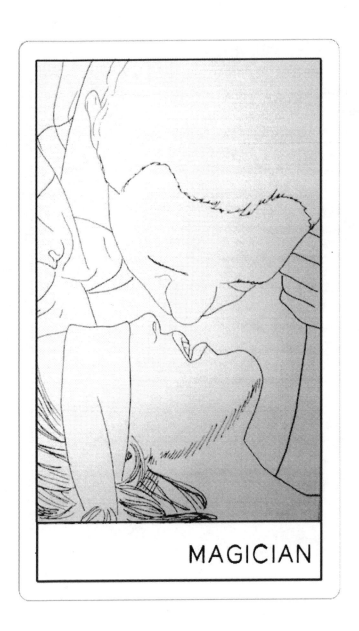

MAGICIAN

# THE MAGICIAN

As you begin your journey, you may question whether or not you're ready for this. The answer: Hell yeah, you are! You have all the tools and resources you need to get started. You are smart, funny, and gosh darnit, people like you. You have the power to make things happen.

**Key Phrase:** Recognize Your True Power
**Astrological Correspondence:** Mercury

**What's Happening:**
- Having all the necessary tools and skills
- Manifesting your intentions
- Handy, good manual skills
- Good at influencing others

**What To Do:**
- Use all your talents and resources
- Use visualization to help manifest your intentions
- Use your gift of gab to talk people into things
- Don't be a con artist

**Questions to Ask Yourself:**
1. What form does passion/creativity take in the situation?
2. What form does emotion/intuition take in the situation?
3. What form does thoughts/communication take in the situation?
4. What form does effort/manifestation take in the situation?
5. How am I currently putting these tools to use?
6. How can I use my tools more effectively?

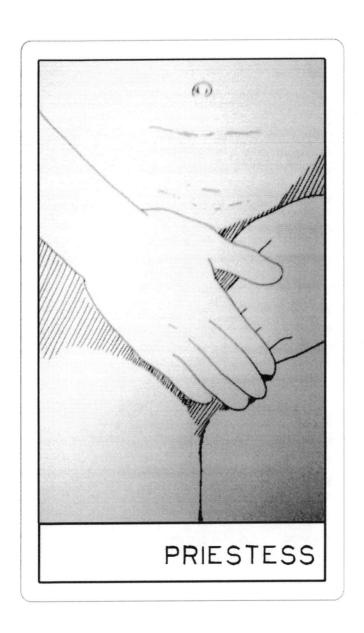

PRIESTESS

# THE HIGH PRIESTESS

Sometimes life throws you for a loop, and you wonder what the hell is going on  and what you should do next. The High Priestess tells you to look within. Listen to your intuition, and figure out what your dreams and hunches are leading you to. You'll get a lot farther by relying on what you already know in your heart than you will by following others.

**Key Phrase:** Listen to your intuition
**Astrological Correspondence:** Moon

**What's Happening:**
- Intuitive hunches
- Prophetic dreams
- Psychic work
- Looking for the perfect woman

**What To Do:**
- Listen to your intuition
- Pay attention to your dreams
- Use your knowledge
- Stop being so harsh or critical

**Questions to Ask Yourself:**
1. What is my inner voice trying to tell me about this situation?
2. Why is my inner voice telling me this?
3. How can I put this suggestion into action?

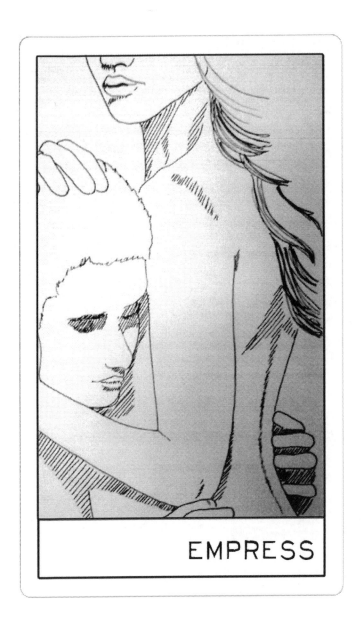

EMPRESS

# THE EMPRESS

You've got feminine wiles at your disposal so use them. You are surrounded by raw creativity and abundance, and you have the power of love in your arsenal. Think about the greatest mom ever: She's caring, nurturing, supportive and can make a damn good meatloaf. And all moms love flowers.

**Key Phrase:** Nurture Creativity
**Astrological Correspondence:** Venus

**What's Happening:**
- Showing empathy and care
- Tapping into your feminine energy
- Your Mother

**What To Do:**
- Use your creativity
- Learn to care and nurture
- Give someone a hug
- Stop nagging

**Questions to Ask Yourself:**
1. What am I in the process of creating?
2. What am I being called to nurture?
3. How can I tap into my motherly instincts in this situation?
4. How can I call upon the abundance of nature in this situation?
5. How will I know when it's time to let go?

EMPEROR

# THE EMPEROR

You have the power to create order out of chaos. When life gives you lemons, you build a lemonade empire unlike anything the world's ever seen. You know how to take control of the situation and put people and resources to good use. More than likely, you are the person people turn to when shit hits the fan.

**Key Phrase:** Make a plan
**Astrological Correspondence:** Aries

**What's Happening:**
- Showing authority
- Dealing with an authority figure
- Creating order out of chaos
- Your Father

**What To Do:**
- Take control of the situation
- Show your own authority
- Follow the law/rules
- Stop being so rigid and inflexible

**Questions to Ask Yourself:**
1. What are the raw materials in the situation?
2. How could these pieces fit together?
3. What do I need to consider in making my plan?
4. How can I create structure in this situation?
5. How can I bring forth my leadership abilities?

HIEROPHANT

# THE HIEROPHANT

Knowledge is power. And when you know things, people tend to listen. This is a time to rely on the things you've learned, as well as the knowledge that others have gained. You would also do well to share that knowledge with less awesome morons. Because that knowledge could help you make some better choices in the future.

**Key Phrase:** Learn from experience
**Astrological Correspondence:** Taurus

**What's Happening:**
- Using your learned knowledge
- Following tradition
- Listening to learned advice
- Sharing what you've learned

**What To Do:**
- Use what you've learned, what you can prove
- Stick to traditions
- Listen to your elders/mentors
- Teach others what you've learned

**Questions to Ask Yourself:**
1. What am I teaching?
2. What am I learning?
3. How am I teaching?
4. How am I learning?
5. How can I improve my teaching?
6. How can I improve my learning?

LOVERS

# THE LOVERS

Life is all about choices. Should you take the the high road, or go for instant gratification? This is one of those times when you'll have to make a choice. Just be sure to choose wisely you won't be able to take it back later. And always remember: Bitches and hoes are fun for a while, but it's a motherfucker trying to turn them into housewives.

**Key Phrase:** Choose wisely
**Astrological Correspondence:** Gemini

**What's Happening:**
- A choice is being presented
- A test or exam
- Meeting your soulmate
- Doing what you're meant to do

**What To Do:**
- Make a choice using your heart
- Take the high road
- Go with the more fulfilling option

**Questions to Ask Yourself:**
1. What is the first option?
2. What is the second option?
3. How would I go after the first option?
4. How would I go after the second option?
5. What would be the result of the first option?
6. What would be the result of the second option?
7. Which option would bring me lasting fulfillment?

CHARIOT

# THE CHARIOT

You've made your choice, and now you're own your way. You've got your shiny new set of wheel, and your turn by turn directions. You know what you want, and where you're going. And you'll be turning heads as you ride by in style and control.

**Key Phrase:** Remain Focused
**Astrological Correspondence:** Cancer

**What's Happening:**
- Knowing your path
- Getting things together
- Making a name for yourself
- Dealing with a car

**What To Do:**
- Figure out where you want to go
- Align your thoughts and emotions
- Recognize your own achievements
- Research when dealing with cars and trips

**Questions to Ask Yourself:**
1. What is the goal that I'm pursuing?
2. How is my solar energy coming forth in this situation?
3. How is my lunar energy coming forth in this situation?
4. How can I create balance between the two energies?
5. How can I use that balance to propel me forward?

STRENGTH

# STRENGTH

We all have our inner beast to contend with, and every once in awhile that little fucker can get slightly out of hand. But with love and courage, and some good ol' inner fortitude, you can tame that beast. Doesn't mean you'll get rid of it completely  you'll just be able to put it on a leash, and maybe sic 'em on people.

**Key Phrase:** Act with compassion
**Astrological Correspondence:** Leo

**What's Happening:**
- Being courageous
- Facing your fears
- Opening your heart
- Lashing out

**What To Do:**
- Be vulnerable
- React with love and compassion
- Face your fears
- Avoid reacting out of fear or anger

**Questions to Ask Yourself:**
1. What form is my inner beast taking in this situation?
2. What form would love and compassion take in this situation?
3. How can I tame my inner beast in this situation?
4. How can I bring more love and compassion into the situation?

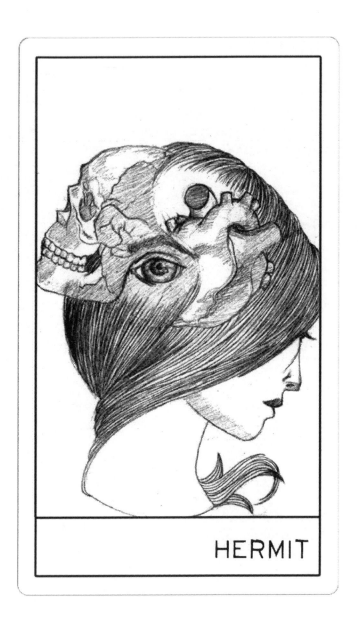

HERMIT

# THE HERMIT

We all need our alone time at one point or another. When you're surrounded by idiots and gold diggers, sometimes it's best to get away from it all and regroup. This would be a time to reflect on your own values and what you hold near and dear, without the interference of others. You never know you may inspire others to do the same.

**Key Phrase:** Follow your wisdom
**Astrological Correspondence:** Virgo

**What's Happening:**
- Isolation or solitude
- Studying or researching
- Contemplating life
- Inspiring others

**What To Do:**
- Take some time for yourself
- Get away from outside influence
- Research and learn
- Contemplate

**Questions to Ask Yourself:**
1. What answer is waiting within me?
2. How have my experiences led me to this answer?
3. How can I follow these answers in this situation?
4. How can I be a guide to others in the situation?

WHEEL

# THE WHEEL OF FORTUNE

Life is a series of cycles. Sometimes you're up, and sometimes you're down. But more than likely, this is one of those times when you're up, or about to get there. But don't just rely on fate and destiny and luck to get you there  work for it yourself. That's usually when luck and opportunity find their way to your doorstep anyway.

**Key Phrase:** Go with the flow
**Astrological Correspondence:** Jupiter

**What's Happening:**
- Good luck
- Unexpected events
- Cyclic behavior
- Learning lessons

**What To Do:**
- Go with the flow
- Create your own luck
- Break the cycle
- Look at the patterns

**Questions to Ask Yourself:**
1. What is going down the wheel in this situation?
2. What is coming up the wheel in this situation?
3. How can I center myself in this situation?

JUSTICE

# JUSTICE

Karma's a bitch  if you rub her the wrong way. Life has a way of rewarding those who do the right thing, and bitchslapping the ones who fuck up. Don't be one of those people. And if one of those people did you wrong, don't worry. They'll get what's coming to them soon enough. Just keep doing you.

**Key Phrase:** Create good karma
**Astrological Correspondence:** Libra

**What's Happening:**
- Karma
- Balance and fairness
- Getting what's deserved
- Legal issues

**What To Do:**
- Watch your own actions
- Take responsibility
- Be fair and unbiased
- Get a lawyer

**Questions to Ask Yourself:**
1. What decision led to this point?
2. What do I need to take responsibility for?
3. What blame should I stop trying to claim?
4. How is karma playing its part in this situation?

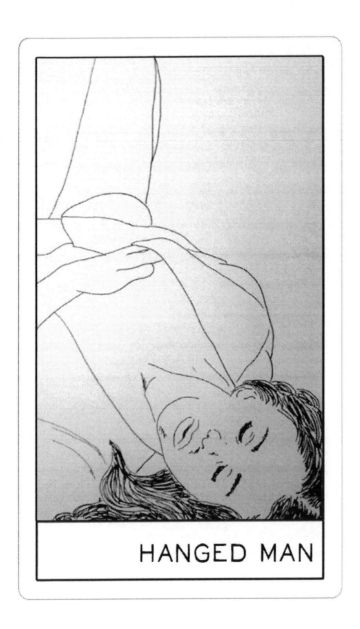

HANGED MAN

# THE HANGED MAN

Sometimes, when things get hectic and you start getting weighed down by the trivial things, it's best to turn yourself and your world  upside down. Sure, everything will fall out of your pockets, but then you get to look at it and figure out if it's really worth carrying around with you. If not, leave it on the ground. Somebody else could probably use it more than you can.

**Key Phrase:** See the big picture
**Astrological Correspondence:** Neptune

**What's Happening:**
- Suspension
- Sacrifice
- A change in perspective
- Being a martyr

**What To Do:**
- Pause and look around
- Get rid of the trivial
- Change your point of view
- Stop giving more than necessary

**Questions to Ask Yourself:**
1. What is trivial in this situation?
2. How is it preventing me from seeing the big picture?
3. What is the other perspective that I'm not seeing?
4. What should I pause or sacrifice?

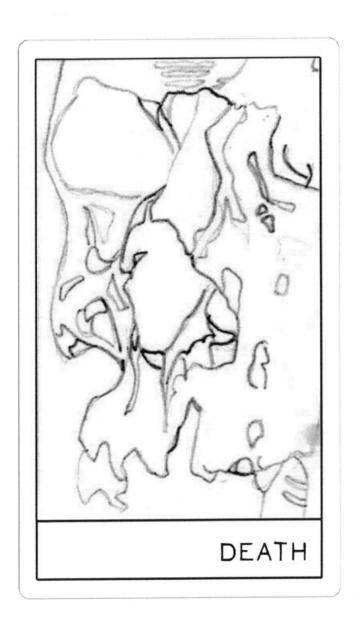

DEATH

# DEATH

Before anything begins, something has to end. You don't start watching one movie while another one is still playing, do you? If you did, you wouldn't really be able to pay attention to either all that well, silly. This is one of those times when you need to let go of the past, so that you can make room for the future. Take out that old VHS  no one even makes those anymore  so that you can start a new chapter. An even better one at that.

**Key Phrase:** Accept Change
**Astrological Correspondence:** Scorpio

**What's Happening:**
- Change
- Losing something old
- Making room for the new
- Fighting change

**What To Do:**
- Get ready for a transformation
- Get rid of what's no longer working
- Clear out some space
- Go with the flow

**Questions to Ask Yourself:**
1. What change is coming?
2. How am I accepting it?
3. How am I blocking it?
4. How can I make room for new things in this situation?

TEMPERANCE

# TEMPERANCE

"Everything in moderation." That's what they always say. Sometimes you need to even things out in order to get shit down. Take a little of this and a dash of that, and you could end up creating something even better than you would have without the combination. All good things require patience. If you're able to adapt and work with others, you'd be surprised at how well things turn out.

**Key Phrase:** Learn to compromise
**Astrological Correspondence:** Sagittarius

**What's Happening:**
- Balance
- Compromise and adaptation
- Healing
- Partnerships

**What To Do:**
- Work with others
- Learn to compromise
- Fine-tune your plans
- Create more balance in your life

**Questions to Ask Yourself:**
1. What are the ideas that I should combine?
2. What aspect do these ideas share?
3. What is the unifying theme behind these ideas?

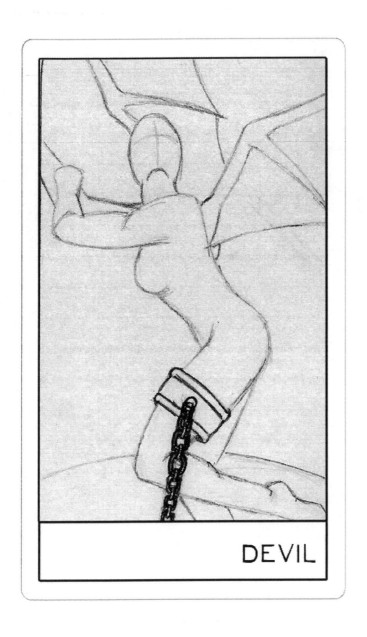

DEVIL

# THE DEVIL

We all have our vices  and who doesn't like to indulge every once in awhile? Smoke, drink, fuck, whatever. It's your life. But the real question is, do you let those things hold you back, or do you acknowledge their place in your life and move forward? Go ahead and be dirty if you want to. But if you can't put down the bottle long enough to pay the bills, maybe you should reconsider how often you let yourself get crazy.

**Key Phrase:** Conquer your ego and fear
**Astrological Correspondence:** Capricorn

**What's Happening:**
- Let fears and vices hold you back
- Indulging in vices
- Blaming external forces for your own doing
- Accepting your inner demons

**What To Do:**
- Lower your inhibitions
- Accept your fears and vices
- Accept responsibility for your actions
- Stop holding back

**Questions to Ask Yourself:**
1. How is my ego holding me back?
2. What fear am I letting control me?
3. How can I confront this fear?
4. What am I doing that's unhealthy?
5. How can I turn this around?

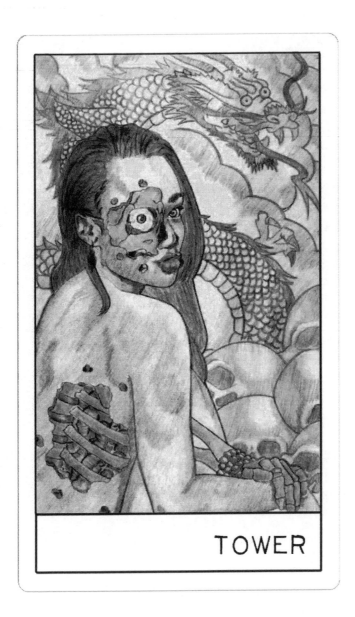

TOWER

# THE TOWER

Shit just got real. You've spent all this time thinking that you were safe and secure, when all you've really done is locked yourself away inside a wobbly castle built on bullshit. And now those walls are coming down, whether you like it or not. Get ready for a shock to your system: all the signs are there, if you'd stop being an ass and pay attention.

**Key Phrase:** Stop pretending
**Astrological Correspondence:** Mars

**What's Happening:**
- Disaster
- A flash of enlightenment
- Unfounded ego
- Hiding behind walls

**What To Do:**
- Look for signs
- Come from behind your walls
- Open up to others
- Examine your foundation

**Questions to Ask Yourself:**
1. What assumption am I making?
2. What am I pretending about?
3. What sign should I be paying attention to?
4. How can I avert future disaster?

STAR

# THE STAR

No matter how dark and dreary things get, there's always hope. All you have to do is look up. This is one of those times when you'll get the encouragement you need to keep on keepin' on  a sign that you're on the right track. Maybe you'll even get some help out of the blue. Just know that if you keep doing what you're doing, you'll make your own wishes come true.

**Key Phrase:** Stay hopeful
**Astrological Correspondence:** Aquarius

**What's Happening:**
- Hope
- Faith
- Unexpected help
- A sign that you're own the right path

**What To Do:**
- Be optimistic
- Be the star in your own show
- Keeping doing what you're doing
- Learn to have faith

**Questions to Ask Yourself:**
1. How can I find hope in this situation?
2. What is the guiding light in this situation?
3. How can I make further progress down my current path?

MOON

# THE MOON

Ever walk through a forest at night? It's easy to get lost: take the wrong path, try to follow the sounds of a bird, or get distracted by some ray of light, and you're fucked. Here's an idea: sit your ass down and go to sleep. Pay attention to your dreams  maybe you'll get a message from your subconscious. Besides, it's much easier to navigate through life when the sun is shining.

**Key Phrase:** Ignore distractions
**Astrological Correspondence:** Pisces

**What's Happening:**
- Distractions
- Illusions
- Deception
- Strange dreams

**What To Do:**
- Listen, but don't act
- Listen to your intuition
- Be wary of the situation
- Pay attention to your dreams

**Questions to Ask Yourself:**
1. What's distracting me in this situation?
2. What is the cause of all the confusion?
3. What's beneath the surface in this situation?
4. What is my intuition trying to tell me about this situation?

SUN

# THE SUN

It's a brand new day! You've fallen, gotten back up and dusted yourself off. And look how far you've come. You can find warmth and beauty in life, and it shows on your face. You have that inner glow of a person that knows what gratitude, love and true friendship really are. And people can see that, and just can't seem to stay away. Because when you're truly happy, you make others happy. And who wouldn't want a piece of that?

**Key Phrase:** Shine your light
**Astrological Correspondence:** Sun

**What's Happening:**
- Joy
- Happiness
- Success
- Recognition

**What To Do:**
- Smile
- Celebrate your happiness
- Accept praise and recognition
- Plan ahead

**Questions to Ask Yourself:**
1. What does success look like for this situation?
2. How can I share joy and warmth in this situation?
3. What does my inner child have to say about this situation?

JUDGEMENT

# JUDGEMENT

Now is the time to look back over your journey. What choices did you make? What sins did you commit? What did you accomplish? Look at your past and dig beneath the surface to figure out the life lessons that you can carry with you. Got it? Good. Now let that shit go. You can't move forward if you keep looking behind you. And you've got places to go and a calling to heed. Your calling. Hop to it.

**Key Phrase:** Heed your higher calling
**Astrological Correspondence:** Pluto

**What's Happening:**
- Rebirth
- Starting a new cycle
- Letting go of the past
- Learning from your past

**What To Do:**
- Accept your decisions
- Move on
- Let go of the past
- Heed your calling

**Questions to Ask Yourself:**
1. What do I need to review in this situation?
2. What do I need to forgive in this situation?
3. What do I need to release?
4. What lesson should I take with me?
5. How can I move forward towards my higher calling?

WORLD

# THE WORLD

Well, alright! You made it! You've lived, you've loved, you've cried and you've sacrificed. You've learned your lessons and you've worked your way to the top. And now, you get to reap the rewards. You've completed the cycle and are well on your way to a new beginning. But for now, celebrate! It's time to break out the happy dance.

**Key Phrase:** Everything comes together
**Astrological Correspondence:** Saturn

**What's Happening:**
- Satisfaction
- Fulfillment
- Being perfectly happy
- Striving for perfection

**What To Do:**
- Rejoice in your success
- Strive for happiness
- Be happy
- Stop trying to be perfect

**Questions to Ask Yourself:**
1. Where did I start in this journey?
2. What did I learn during this journey?
3. What success am I celebrating?
4. How can I take my lessons with me into the next cycle?

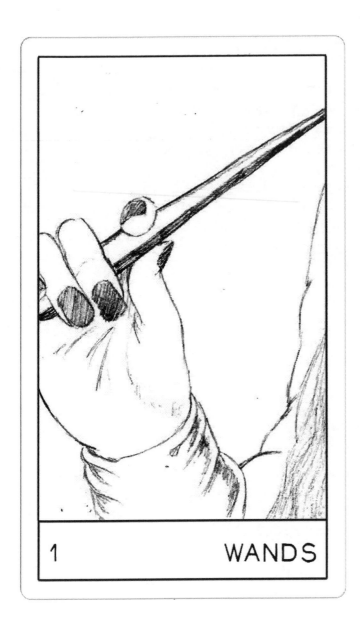

1                    WANDS

## WANDS

Wands are the fire suit of the tarot. They are all about energy, movement, and passion. They tend to represent career, creativity, and things that you are enthusiastic about.

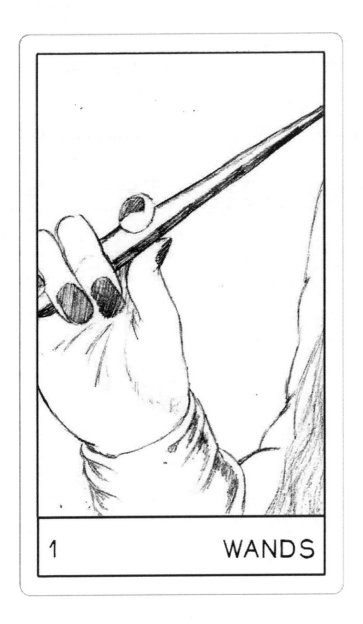

1          WANDS

# ACE OF WANDS

This is the spark that ignites the flame. You're feeling inspired, creative and full of enthusiasm. You've got a new idea that you are just dying to start working on. Use that energy to get started.

**Key Phrase:** Creative spark
**Astrological Correspondence:** Fire Signs

**What's Happening:**
- New idea
- New spark
- Enthusiasm
- Burnout

**What To Do:**
- Follow your inspiration
- Take action
- Be enthusiastic
- Pace yourself

**Questions to Ask Yourself:**
1. What's the new passion in the situation?
2. What would be the greatest good of this passion?
3. How can I create sustainable progress with it?
4. How can I avoid overdoing it?

2                 WANDS

# TWO OF WANDS

Decisions, decisions... Do you stick to what you know, and stay safe where you are, or do you take a leap of faith and try something new? This is the time to make that choice: Do you stay, or do you go?

**Key Phrase:** Choose your path
**Astrological Correspondence:** Mars in Aries

**What's Happening:**
- Making a decision
- Going out on a limb
- Trying something new
- Sticking to the tried and true

**What To Do:**
- Make a choice
- Try something new
- Break with routine
- Stick to what you know

**Questions to Ask Yourself:**
1. What is tried and true in this situation?
2. What would a new path look like?
3. How can I be true to myself in this situation?

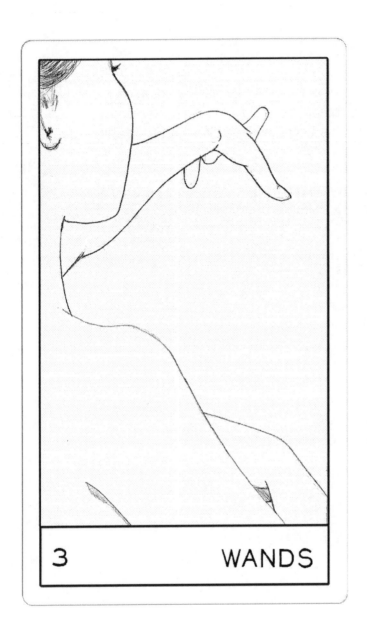

3              WANDS

# THREE OF WANDS

Things are looking good. You've done the initial work and put yourself out there. You've made samples, written emails and shown people who you are and what you can do. And you're proud of yourself. Now, you just have to wait and see what people think.

**Key Phrase:** Expand your horizons
**Astrological Correspondence:** Sun in Aries

**What's Happening:**
- Putting yourself out there
- Showing your work
- Paying for something
- Being ambitious

**What To Do:**
- Pull your resources together
- Present your skills and talents
- Polish up your resume
- Tweak your work

**Questions to Ask Yourself:**
1. What choice has brought me to this point?
2. How am I expressing my worth?
3. How am I expanding in this situation?
4. How will I know when my ship has come in?

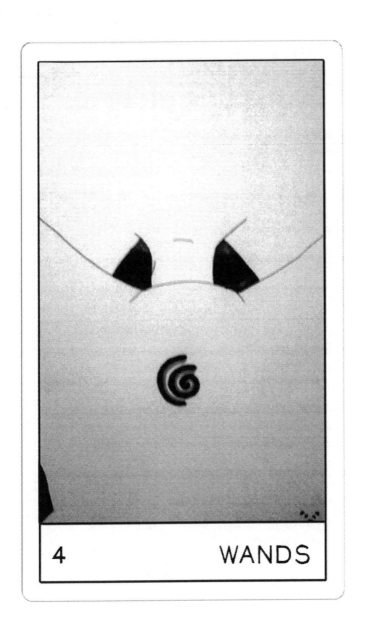

4                    WANDS

# FOUR OF WANDS

Huzzah! It's the first taste of success. You've build a damn fine foundation for yourself, with all that work and energy you put into the beginning of this endeavor. And now you're seeing the initial benefits. There's still a whole lotta work to be done, but for right now, it's a celebration, bitches! Take some time to pat yourself on the back.

**Key Phrase:** Celebrate initial success
**Astrological Correspondence:** Venus in Aries

**What's Happening:**
- A new relationship
- The first milestone
- Building a solid foundation
- Celebrating success

**What To Do:**
- Celebrate your initial success
- Create a solid foundation
- Recognize your progress
- Get back to work

**Questions to Ask Yourself:**
1. What success am I enjoying?
2. What how did I get to this point?
3. How can I sustain this initial success in the future?

5         WANDS

# FIVE OF WANDS

Looks like someone is butting heads. But a little passionate debating never hurt anyone. Things are getting a tad bit competitive amongst your peers. That's okay. But just like you want your opinion to be heard, so does everyone else. Try to listen at least as much as you talk, and things will be just fine.

**Key Phrase:** Friendly competition
**Astrological Correspondence:** Saturn in Leo

**What's Happening:**
- Competition
- Debate
- Bickering among friends
- Brainstorming ideas

**What To Do:**
- Listen to everyone's input
- Speak your mind
- Pick your battles
- Find a way to stand out

**Questions to Ask Yourself:**
1. How can I avoid creating unnecessary conflict?
2. How can I embrace the different points of view?
3. How can I stand out and be heard?

6　　　　　　　　WANDS

# SIX OF WANDS

Check out that sweet, sweet victory. You've won! You've conquered your obstacles and bested your rivals, and now the crowd loves you. It's a good feeling. Just don't let it go to your head. Remember how you got there, or those rivals may come back to bite you in the ass. And not in a sexy kind of way.

**Key Phrase:** Accept victory graciously
**Astrological Correspondence:** Jupiter in Leo

**What's Happening:**
- Success
- Recognition
- Reward
- Getting a big head

**What To Do:**
- Give yourself more credit
- Accept your rewards
- Change your perception of yourself
- Remember how you got there

**Questions to Ask Yourself:**
1. What am I being honored for?
2. What am I letting go to my head?
3. Where am I being called to lead?
4. How can I accept this honor graciously?
5. How can I protect myself from getting knocked down?

7　　　　　　　　WANDS

# SEVEN OF WANDS

Dammit! Just when you thought you were on top of things, you turn around and find people poking at you, trying to knock off your crown. You've got some folks riding your ass, trying to get to where you are. The best way to deal with that is to stand your ground, and be the same person that got to the top in the first place.

**Key Phrase:** Defend your beliefs
**Astrological Correspondence:** Mars in Leo

**What's Happening:**
- Being attacked
- Getting defensive
- Maintaining your success
- Guarding your status

**What To Do:**
- Be transparent
- Be authentic
- Show your intentions
- Do what you did to get to where you are

**Questions to Ask Yourself:**
1. What beliefs am I standing up for?
2. Are these beliefs serving my highest good?
3. How can I remain on higher ground?
4. What beliefs could I let go of?
5. How will I be validated in my beliefs?

8          WANDS

# EIGHT OF WANDS

Time flies when you're having fun. And things are moving at the speed of sound right now. The power of your intentions and the passion behind your goals are propelling you forward, so use this energy to get shit done. You may find that it's a whole lot easier than usual to knock out your proverbial todo list.

**Key Phrase:** Quick manifestation
**Astrological Correspondence:** Mercury in Sagittarius

**What's Happening:**
- Lots of energy
- Getting a lot done
- Moving quickly
- Moving too quickly

**What To Do:**
- Make a plan
- Use the energy to get things done
- Focus on your ideas and intentions
- Slow down and focus

**Questions to Ask Yourself:**
1. What is manifesting in this situation?
2. How did I bring this into being?
3. What intentions created this situation?
4. How can I prepare for the situation?
5. How can I keep up with the situation?

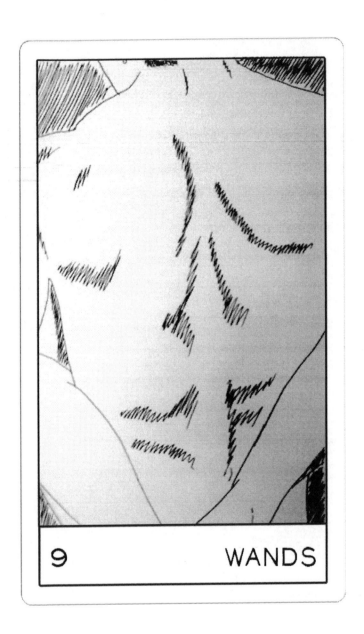

9          WANDS

# NINE OF WANDS

You're tired. You've done a lot of work, and you've done a damn good job at it. You've gotten some bumps and bruises and taken some knocks along the way, but so far things are looking good. But you're so tired. Don't worry you're almost at the end. This is the time to give it one last push.

**Key Phrase:** Last ditch effort
**Astrological Correspondence:** Moon in Sagittarius

**What's Happening:**
- The last hurdle
- Being tired but proud
- Working through obstacles
- Displaying your work

**What To Do:**
- Keep going
- Ask for help
- Stay the course
- Take pride in what you've done

**Questions to Ask Yourself:**
1. Where do I stand now?
2. How has my past experiences gotten me to this point?
3. What am I trying to protect?
4. How is my caution blocking growth?
5. How can I make the final push to success?

10       WANDS

# TEN OF WANDS

Now you've done it. You're the boss. You've made it to the top, and you can say that you've done it your way. Yet things don't seem as fun as you thought they'd be. That's because you're doing all the work. You've taken on all the responsibilities, and it's making you lose sight of why you started out in the first place. The best way not to completely lose your passion and enthusiasm? Drop some of those responsibilities onto someone else's shoulders. Lighten your load, and you'll be able to get a better view of the horizon.

**Key Phrase:** Burdened by success
**Astrological Correspondence:** Saturn in Sagittarius

**What's Happening:**
- Burdened by success
- Burnout
- Trying to do it all
- Not trusting others' abilities

**What To Do:**
- Reconnect with your passion
- Delegate
- Prioritize
- Ask for help

**Questions to Ask Yourself:**
1. What success have I created?
2. How is it overburdening me?
3. What is my top priority in this situation?
4. What could I do away with?
5. Who could I ask for help?
6. How can I avoid burnout?

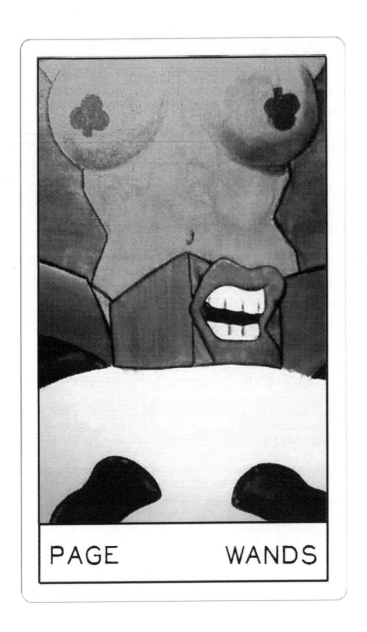

PAGE          WANDS

# PAGE OF WANDS

This is free-spirited little fucker. He's full of vim and vigor, enthusiasm and pizazz. He may come to you bearing a message of some sort: It'll be out of the blue, but it will rock your world, in a good way. He's the one that brings all kinds of youthful inspiration those pie-in-the-sky ideas that, if given a bit of thought and planning, just might work.

**Key Phrase:** Eager to get started
**Astrological Correspondence:** Spring

**What's Happening:**
- A new idea
- An inspirational message
- An unexpected surprise
- An inspiring, but naive person

**What To Do:**
- Pursue the idea
- Pay attention to signs and messages
- Be enthusiastic
- Be realistic

**Questions to Ask Yourself:**
1. What am I so excited about?
2. How can I take the first step to get started?
3. How can I create sustainable progress with it?

KNIGHT     WANDS

# KNIGHT OF WANDS

This is the guy that takes the idea and runs with it, full force. He's impulsive and passionate, and will charge full speed ahead when he's inspired enough. The only problem is, sometimes he misses some things while he's hurrying off. Plus, most of the time, he doesn't even have a game plan  he's just winging it. It could get him in trouble, but more than likely people will be so enamored with his enthusiasm that they'll help him along the way.

**Key Phrase:** Rushing to glory
**Astrological Correspondence:** Sagittarius

**What's Happening:**
- Taking off
- Moving forward quickly
- Showing passion
- Missing out on the details

**What To Do:**
- Go for it!
- Act quickly
- Take advantage of the opportunity
- Slow down and plan things out

**Questions to Ask Yourself:**
1. What is my end goal?
2. How is my enthusiasm influencing others?
3. How can I convince others to help me in this situation?
4. What pitfalls should I look out for?
5. What would I miss by not slowing down?

QUEEN　　　WANDS

# QUEEN OF WANDS

This is one fiery woman. She's full of warmth and confidence, and she knows how to work a room like she owns it. She's creative and inspiring, and she knows how to encourage and motivate the many people that gravitate towards her. She does have a temper, and she can flip her bitch switch at any moment. But it won't take long for her to calm down. Hell, that's one of the reasons people love her so much.

**Key Phrase:** Seductive enthusiasm
**Astrological Correspondence:** Aries

**What's Happening:**
- Honesty
- Confidence
- Sexual attraction
- Being moody

**What To Do:**
- Use your passion
- Share your ideas
- Use your sex appeal
- Be creative

**Questions to Ask Yourself:**
1. How do I express my passion in this situation?
2. How can I draw on my sensuality?
3. How can I use my creativity in this situation?
4. How can I fascinate those around me?

KING     WANDS

# KING OF WANDS

This is the natural born leader. He's creative and entrepreneurial, and he knows how to get shit done. Well, it's more like, he has a vision of what needs to be done, and he knows how to get other people to do it. He's the guy that orchestrated the operation, then supervises. And people are cool with that, because he seems to see what no one else can. He's just awesome like that.

**Key Phrase:** Creative supervisor
**Astrological Correspondence:** Leo

**What's Happening:**
- Being a visionary
- Sharing ideas
- Making things happen
- Being quiet

**What To Do:**
- Share your vision with others
- Work with others to make things happen
- Enlist the skills of others
- Use your entrepreneurial spirit

**Questions to Ask Yourself:**
1. What am I getting others excited about?
2. How is my passion making me a good leader?
3. What risk is my gut urging me to take?
4. How can I become a better leader in this situation?

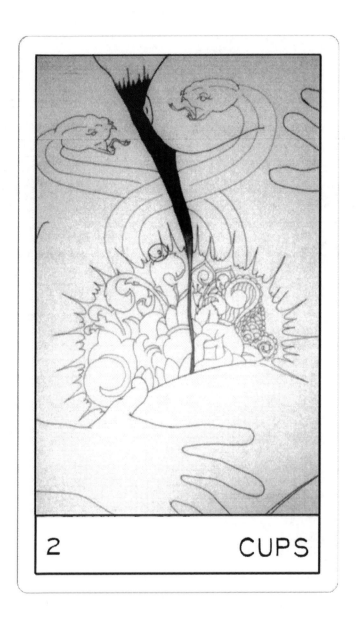

## CUPS

Cups are the water suit. They signal emotions, artistic tendencies and intuition. Cups represent relationships, creative endeavors, and things that make you feel mushy.

1                    CUPS

# ACE OF CUPS

Ah, new love. Isn't it grand? You're filled with seemingly overwhelming emotion right now. You're feeling creative and intuitive, like you could just give the world a hug. Take that new sense of love and run with it.

**Key Phrase:** New love
**Astrological Correspondence:** Water Signs

**What's Happening:**
- New love
- New abundance
- The potential for a new relationship
- Wanting too much too soon

**What To Do:**
- Open your heart
- Accept joy and abundance
- Be receptive
- Slow down

**Questions to Ask Yourself:**
1. What's the new love in the situation?
2. What would be the greatest good of this opportunity?
3. How can I create sustainable progress with it?
4. How can I avoid overdoing it?

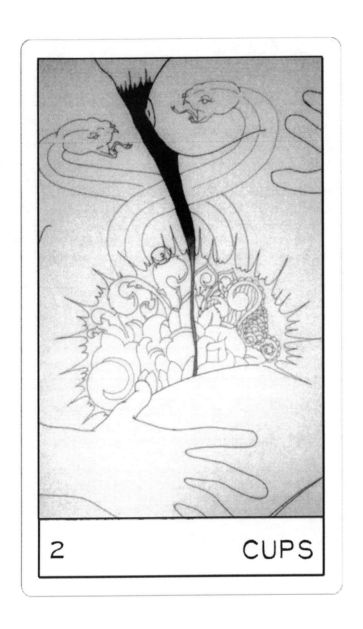

2          CUPS

# TWO OF CUPS

Looks like someone has a new playmate. Someone new has entered your life, and it's giving your butterflies. A new friend, a new partner, a new romantic interest perhaps? Put on your happy pants because this new relationship will be joyful and mutually beneficial. Go hold hands and skip.

**Key Phrase:** Mutual attraction
**Astrological Correspondence:** Venus in Cancer

**What's Happening:**
- New relationship
- Compromise
- New level of commitment
- Breakup

**What To Do:**
- Be approachable
- Introduce yourself
- Learn to work together with others
- Do your share of the work

**Questions to Ask Yourself:**
1. Who or what  am I attracted to in this situation?
2. What benefit would I gain?
3. What benefit am I giving?
4. How can I make this new relationship last?

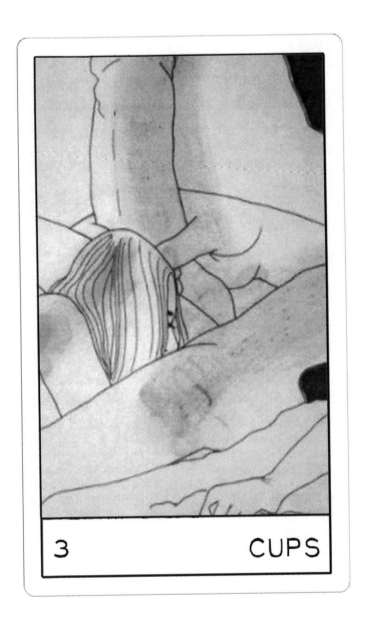

# THREE OF CUPS

It's a celebration, bitches! A group or community of some sort has taken you into the fold and everyone's happy. Everyone's feeling the love and passing the booze. This is a time for joy and laughter, for hanging out with good friends, good food, and good music.

**Key Phrase:** Joyous gatherings
**Astrological Correspondence:** Mercury in Cancer

**What's Happening:**
- Celebration
- Acceptance into a community
- Working with peers
- Indulgence

**What To Do:**
- Accept the invitation
- Be part of the community
- Listen to offers for help
- Indulge in moderation

**Questions to Ask Yourself:**
1. What kind of group am I joining?
2. What is the emotional connection there?
3. What joy am I celebrating with this group?
4. How can I avoid overdoing it?

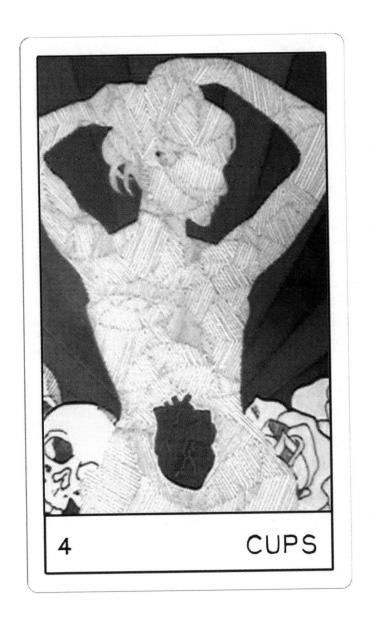

4          CUPS

# FOUR OF CUPS

You've got that 'woe is me' look on your face. Suddenly, things aren't as fun as they used to be. In fact, they seem downright boring. You're looking at what you've obtained, and wondering if you can do better. Well, you can! The Universe is showing you the way. You just need to get your head out of your ass and pay attention.

**Key Phrase:** Grass is greener
**Astrological Correspondence:** Moon in Cancer

**What's Happening:**
- Boredom
- Trying to find excitement
- Looking at what you've got
- Not seeing a new opportunity

**What To Do:**
- Look at what you've done
- Do something to recharge
- Stop standing in your own way
- Pay attention to signs and messages

**Questions to Ask Yourself:**
1. What am I apathetic about in this situation?
2. What am I bored with?
3. What opportunity is waiting for me?
4. What new emotion would this opportunity bring to my life?
5. How can I look up and accept this gift?

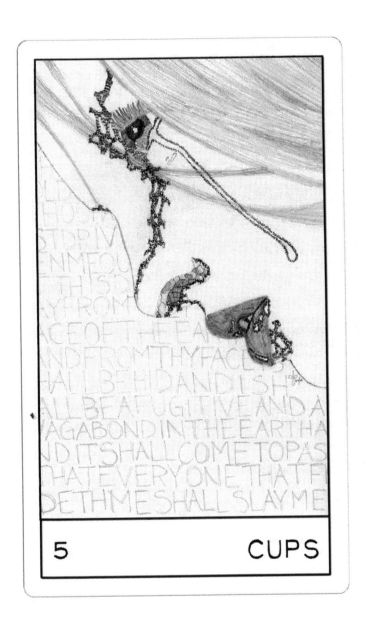

5          CUPS

# FIVE OF CUPS

So you've lost something you loved. A relationship, an opportunity some kind of investment of your energy and emotion. It's just so sad. Whatever should you do? Stop whining like a little bitch! You still have love to give and receive. You still have plenty of creative potential. Stop crying over spilt milk and move on.

**Key Phrase:** Crying over spilt milk
**Astrological Correspondence:** Mars in Scorpio

**What's Happening:**
- Misery
- Missing what you've lost
- A failed relationship
- A failed project

**What To Do:**
- Look at what you still have
- Stop crying over spilt milk
- Let go of the past
- Look for other opportunities

**Questions to Ask Yourself:**
1. What have I lost in this situation?
2. How can I move on from the grief?
3. What potential do I have in front of me?
4. How can I take advantage of that potential?

6                           CUPS

# SIX OF CUPS

You'd be surprised at how much joy you can find in the simple things in life. Just like little children, taking time to enjoy the little things can be a breath of fresh air. You may even run into something or someone that reminds you of the simpler times. Take that feeling and use it in the present. Just don't get caught up in the past.

**Key Phrase:** Innocent Simplicity
**Astrological Correspondence:** Sun in Scorpio

**What's Happening:**
- Nostalgia
- A relationship from the past
- Enjoying simple pleasures
- Being stuck in the past

**What To Do:**
- Look for clues in memories
- Rekindle old feelings
- Keep things simple
- Use the past to thrive in the future

**Questions to Ask Yourself:**
1. How is my past affecting my present?
2. How is this benefiting me now?
3. What lesson can I learn from my past?
4. How can I bring more simplicity into my life?

7  CUPS

# SEVEN OF CUPS

Life is all about choices. But what do you do when you have too many of them? It happens to the best of us. The best thing you can do take a look at your skills and resources, and choose based on reality. Because what may look like a bunch of choices could be your imagination feeding you a bunch of bullshit.

**Key Phrase:** Paralyzed by choice
**Astrological Correspondence:** Venus in Scorpio

**What's Happening:**
- Too many options
- Daydreaming
- Being unrealistic
- Trouble making a choice

**What To Do:**
- Choose based on your resources
- Consider all your options
- Make a choice
- Pay attention to dreams

**Questions to Ask Yourself:**
1. What choices am I faced with?
2. What would be the best case scenario?
3. What would be the worst case scenario?
4. What would be the best option to choose?

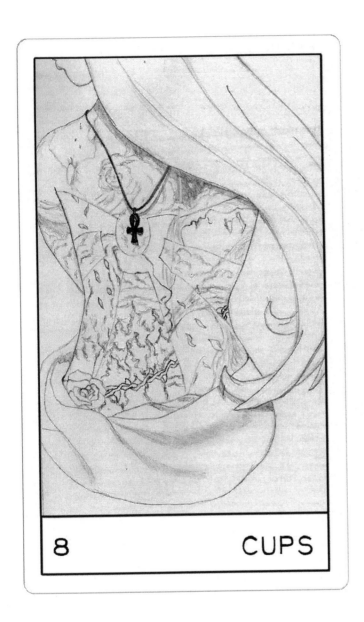

8 CUPS

# EIGHT OF CUPS

You are totally done. You've invested your time, effort and love into a situation, and you've finally reached your limit for bullshit. You can't do anything else to help the situation, and it's now just a waste of time and energy. This would be the time to put your house in order, pack your shit and move on to higher ground. You can do so much better.

**Key Phrase:** Ready to move on
**Astrological Correspondence:** Saturn in Pisces

**What's Happening:**
- Moving on
- Leaving an unworthy situation
- Going for higher ground
- Not knowing when to leave

**What To Do:**
- Put things in order
- Stop wasting your investments
- Save your energy for something better
- Follow your heart to better things

**Questions to Ask Yourself:**
1. What situation is at an end?
2. How can I tie up loose ends emotionally?
3. What am I being called to move toward?

9       CUPS

# NINE OF CUPS

Yippie!! Jackpot, baby! You've lived and loved and put out a shitload of positive vibrations. And now you're being rewarded. You've gotten all that you could wish for, and you are as happy as a pig in shit. Funny thing is, you made it happen. So enjoy!

**Key Phrase:** Gratification
**Astrological Correspondence:** Jupiter in Pisces

**What's Happening:**
- A wish come true
- Satisfaction
- Good health
- Expecting things to fall into your lap

**What To Do:**
- Celebrate your good fortune
- Share your fortune with others
- Work towards your goals
- Appreciate what you have

**Questions to Ask Yourself:**
1. What am I wishing for?
2. Is my wish aligned with my greatest good?
3. How am I manifesting my desires?
4. How can I make my wish come true?

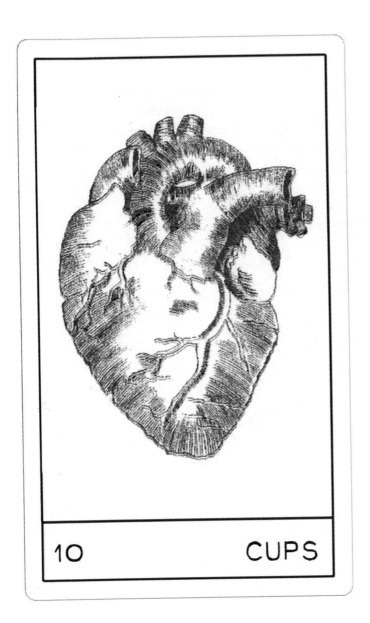

10        CUPS

# TEN OF CUPS

Look at you, enjoying your own happily ever after moment. Not only are you with the people that you want in your life, but you have everything that you could ever dream of: love, a nice home, food on the table, and happy fun times with the kiddies. Life is grand when you can share your good fortune with those you love.

**Key Phrase:** Shared love and joy
**Astrological Correspondence:** Mars in Pisces

**What's Happening:**
- Happiness
- Good times with family
- Harmony
- Something in the way of fulfillment

**What To Do:**
- Celebrate your happiness
- Share your happiness with others
- Spend time with family
- Appreciate what you have

**Questions to Ask Yourself:**
1. What fantasy am I holding onto?
2. How is that stopping me from appreciating what I have now?
3. How can I embrace the love that's around me?
4. How can I share more of my love with others?
5. What joy am I celebrating?
6. How can I share this joy with those around me?
7. How can I sustain this happily ever after?

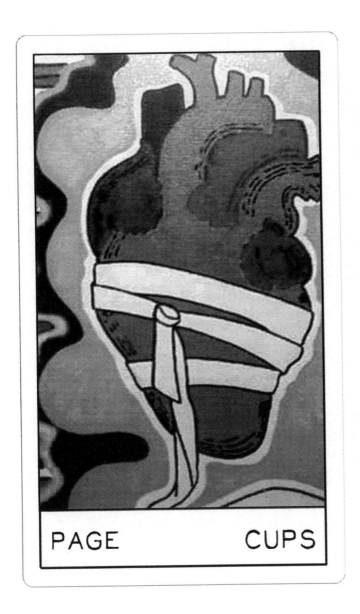

PAGE                    CUPS

# PAGE OF CUPS

This Prince Charming usually comes bearing some surprising inspiration. He's the one that pulls the most creative ideas out of his ass, then gives them to you. And he always seems to show up at just the right moment, when the Moon is in the seventh house and Jupiter aligns with Mars. (Don't worry  he'll most likely know what the hell that means.)

**Key Phrase:** Messages from the heart
**Astrological Correspondence:** Summer

**What's Happening:**
- Inspiration
- A romantic message
- Getting new ideas
- A romantic young person

**What To Do:**
- Listen to your intuition
- Follow your inspiration
- Stay grounded
- Control your emotions

**Questions to Ask Yourself:**
1. How am I sharing my dreams and visions with the world?
2. How am I opening my heart to love?
3. What message is coming my way?

KNIGHT                    CUPS

# KNIGHT OF CUPS

Meet the Ladies' Man. He's suave and smooth and charming and sweet. He's the romantic guy who will bring you flowers and write you cute little text messages. He'll charm the pants off of you. But more than likely, he'll be done after that, and off to his next adventure. He's the guy that follows his heart and searches for the things that connect with his soul. Just be careful that he doesn't break your heart in the process.

**Key Phrase:** Following your heart
**Astrological Correspondence:** Pisces

**What's Happening:**
- Following your heart
- Going after a far-away goal
- Getting distracted
- Going after your heart's desire

**What To Do:**
- Follow your heart
- Pursue your inspiration
- Stay focused on your goal
- Be wary of snake charmers

**Questions to Ask Yourself:**
1. What dream am I moving towards?
2. How am I being distracted in my quest?
3. What relationships am I creating?
4. How can I avoid hurting others in my journey?
5. How is my heart leading me to my goal?

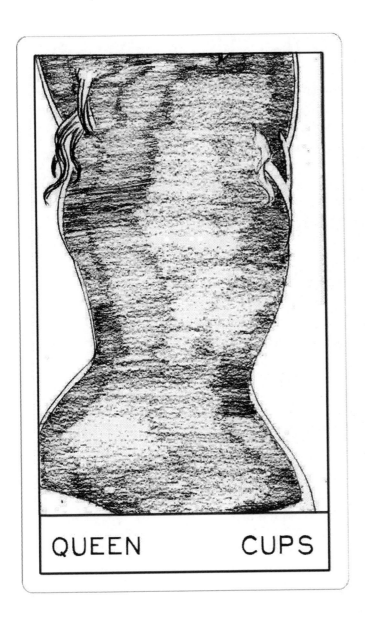

QUEEN       CUPS

# QUEEN OF CUPS

She's the doting mother, the one that seems to have eyes in the back of her head. She's the philanthropist that can't turn a blind eye to a bleeding heart. She loves openly and honestly, because she pulls that love from her soul. She's highly intuitive and can sometimes weird people out with her psychic hunches. Sometimes she can get needy and overly emotional, but mostly she's just a modern-day Mother Theresa.

**Key Phrase:** Seeing into the heart
**Astrological Correspondence:** Cancer

**What's Happening:**
- Being intuitive
- Being empathetic
- Supporting creativity
- Being overly emotional

**What To Do:**
- Use your intuition
- Connect with others emotionally
- Use your artistic talents
- Learn to contain your emotions

**Questions to Ask Yourself:**
1. How can I use my intuition in this situation?
2. What should I be empathetic towards?
3. How can I connect with this situation on an emotional level?
4. How would being more vulnerable help in this situation?

KING                    CUPS

# KING OF CUPS

This guy is cool, calm and collected. He can handle emotions because he has complete control over his own. He's not ashamed or embarrassed to talk about his feelings but you'll probably be the one pouring yours out to him. He makes people feel comfortable because he's so composed. He's also extremely generous, and will probably give you a cookie or the rest of the day off if you cry a little. Just be careful on a bad day, he could use those emotional displays against you to get what he wants.

**Key Phrase:** Emotional maturity
**Astrological Correspondence:** Scorpio

**What's Happening:**
- Being emotionally stable
- Controlling your feelings
- Giving guidance
- Being manipulative

**What To Do:**
- Stay calm
- Be understanding
- Talk about your feelings
- Stay in control of your emotions

**Questions to Ask Yourself:**
1. How have I matured emotionally?
2. How does that maturity allow me to help others?
3. How can I show emotion in a mature way?
4. How can I help others understand their emotions?

1  SWORDS

## SWORDS

Swords represent air in tarot. They are associated with intellect, logic and communication. They talk about your thoughts, how you communicate with people, and things that give you a headache.

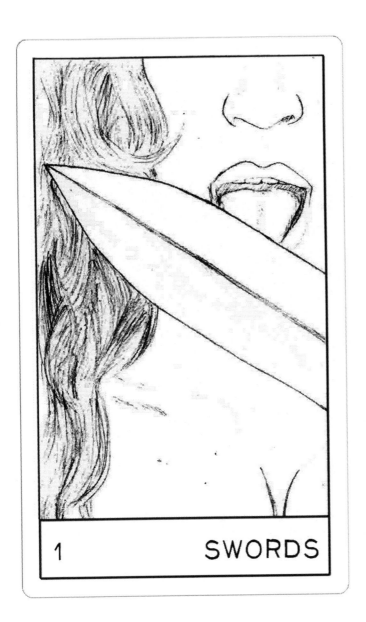

# ACE OF SWORDS

This is like a flash of lighting to your world. You can see the light, and there's a sharp picture in your mind. All the bullshit has been stripped away, so that you have a crystal clear image of the opportunity that is ready to be seized. Just be careful not to cut yourself in the process  make a plan, Stan.

**Key Phrase:** Clear ideas
**Astrological Correspondence:** Air Signs

**What's Happening:**
- New idea
- New clarity
- Getting clear on things
- Being harsh

**What To Do:**
- Get to the heart of the matter
- Make a plan
- Cut through all the B.S.
- Be nice when telling the truth

**Questions to Ask Yourself:**
1. What's the new insight in the situation?
2. What would be the greatest good of this opportunity?
3. How can I make a plan around this new insight?
4. How can I cut away what's not needed?

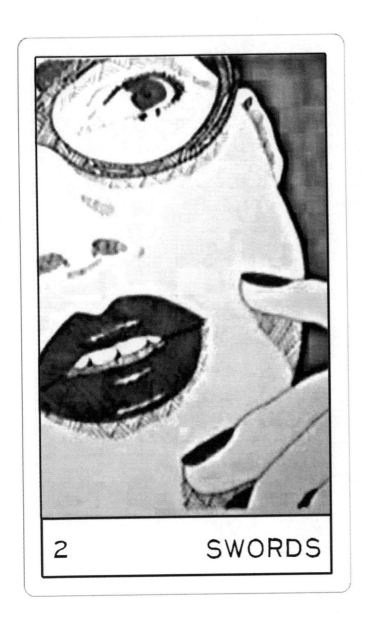

# TWO OF SWORDS

More decisions. Only this time, you've been going back and forth in your head, trying to figure out which option is best for you. You've made pro/con lists, weighed both options from a logical standpoint. And yet you still can't choose. That's because you're not seeing the whole picture: You're missing the part that you would see with your heart. Stop trying to reason everything out and let your intuition decide for you.

**Key Phrase:** Blinded by thoughts
**Astrological Correspondence:** Moon in Libra

**What's Happening:**
- Deadlocked on a decision
- Trying to weigh the pros and cons
- Not using your intuition
- Not having all the facts

**What To Do:**
- Use your intuition
- Look at all the facts
- Get out of your head
- Choose the option that feels best

**Questions to Ask Yourself:**
1. What decision am I being called to make?
2. What's the left sword?
3. What's the right sword??
4. What am I not seeing about this decision?

3          SWORDS

# THREE OF SWORDS

They say that three's a crowd, and in this case, that is not a good thing. Something or someone is going to end up getting neglected and feeling jealous. And that's when the shit starts the hit the fan. Your best bet would be to let something go. It may hurt at first, but that's just something you'll have to go through now to avoid greater pains later.

**Key Phrase:** Painful rejection
**Astrological Correspondence:** Saturn in Libra

**What's Happening:**
- A love triangle
- Pain and confusion
- Arguments
- Ending a relationship

**What To Do:**
- Let go of what's causing pain
- Mourn the loss
- Let from the experience
- Look for a solution

**Questions to Ask Yourself:**
1. What choice is being made in this situation?
2. How will it affect me?
3. How will it affect those around me?
4. How can I do what's best for me in this situation?
5. How can I minimize the pain caused by this choice?

4        SWORDS

# FOUR OF SWORDS

You've come a long way. You've gone through some ups and downs. You've faced heartache and pain. Now it's time to take a break. Pop a squat and rest your head for a minute. Think about how far you've come and what you've learned. Then make a game plan for the future. Whatever you do, just take a load off for awhile. You need it.

**Key Phrase:** Rest and reflect
**Astrological Correspondence:** Jupiter in Libra

**What's Happening:**
- Taking a break
- Thinking about what's happened
- Making a plan
- Getting back in the game

**What To Do:**
- Stop and rest
- Meditate
- Look at what's happened
- Apply past experiences to the present/future

**Questions to Ask Yourself:**
1. How did I get to where I am now?
2. Where am I going in the future?
3. What lessons should I observe from my past experiences?
4. How can I use those lessons to plan for the future?

5 SWORDS

# FIVE OF SWORDS

Some people are just not worth having around. Whether you have a point that you're standing firm on, or you're trying in vain to get some idiot to see your side of things, some causes are just not worth getting your panties in a bunch over. Choose your battles, and learn to compromise, or even agree to disagree. If not, you could just end up alone.

**Key Phrase:** Pick your battles
**Astrological Correspondence:** Venus in Aquarius

**What's Happening:**
- Arguments
- Bickering and infighting
- Pettiness
- Standing up for yourself

**What To Do:**
- Pick your battles wisely
- Walk away
- Agree to disagree
- Learn to compromise

**Questions to Ask Yourself:**
1. What is this conflict about?
2. What are my thoughts on it?
3. What are their thoughts on it?
4. Should I let it go or stand my ground?

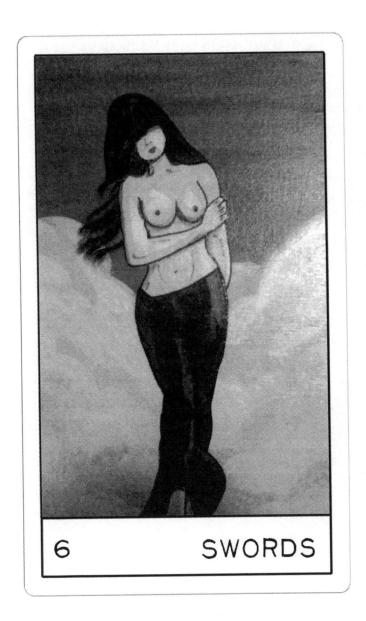

6        SWORDS

# SIX OF SWORDS

Maybe you don't want to abandon all hope, but you know it's time to go. There's too much confusion going on, and people are bickering and kicking up dust about the dumbest shit. It's time for you to move to a more peaceful environment.

**Key Phrase:** Leaving confusion behind
**Astrological Correspondence:** Mercury in Aquarius

**What's Happening:**
- Moving to a more peaceful environment
- Finding answers
- Changing residence
- Going on a trip

**What To Do:**
- Change your surroundings
- Leave confusion behind
- Strike out on your own
- Pack up your things

**Questions to Ask Yourself:**
1. What confusion am I leaving behind?
2. How can I let go of it as I move forward?
3. How can I minimize the pain caused by this situation?
4. What clarity will I find on the other side?

7  SWORDS

# SEVEN OF SWORDS

You've got some secret plans going on, some clandestine activities and tricks up sleeve. Well, if you're going to do it alone, you won't be able to carry everything. You'll have to leave something behind. And that something may be the thing that gets you caught red-handed. Considered yourself warned.

**Key Phrase:** Going it alone
**Astrological Correspondence:** Moon in Aquarius

**What's Happening:**
- Dishonesty
- Doing things alone
- Lying
- Looking out for yourself

**What To Do:**
- Leave what you don't need behind
- Be honest
- Take responsibility for your actions
- Tell the truth

**Questions to Ask Yourself:**
1. What am I trying to achieve?
2. What idea am I taking with me?
3. What idea am I leaving behind?
4. How can I avoid harming others?

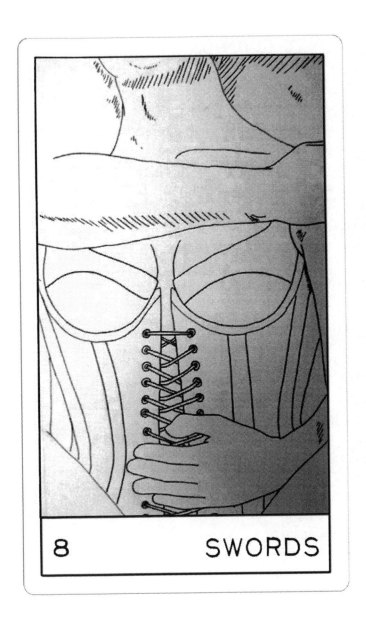

# EIGHT OF SWORDS

You're feeling trapped, locked in place, unable to move backwards, forwards or even sideways. There's a huge obstacle blocking your path  or is there? If you look at it, maybe it's just a bunch of smaller obstacles. And maybe if you take things one step at a time and stop making a mountain out of a molehill, you'll be able to move forward. But the first step is to change your attitude and put some pep in your step.

**Key Phrase:** Limiting beliefs
**Astrological Correspondence:** Jupiter in Gemini

**What's Happening:**
- Feeling trapped
- Getting overwhelmed
- Overexaggerating
- Letting fear of the unknown hold you back

**What To Do:**
- Break the situation down
- Take things one step at a time
- Put things into perspective
- Be courageous and take the first step

**Questions to Ask Yourself:**
1. Where am I trying to go?
2. What am I afraid of?
3. How am I holding myself back?
4. How can I transform my limiting beliefs?
5. What could I do right now to take the first step forward?

9       SWORDS

# NINE OF SWORDS

You worry too much. You spend your nights tossing and turning in bed, or pacing a groove in the floor, wondering if everything will be okay. Did you do the right thing? Did you do it well enough? Are things going to work out? Calm down! Things aren't as bad as they seem  and worrying doesn't change a damn thing anyway. Go to sleep, silly.

**Key Phrase:** Paranoid overthinking
**Astrological Correspondence:** Mars in Gemini

**What's Happening:**
- Paranoia
- Worrying too much
- Losing sleep
- Being too hard on yourself

**What To Do:**
- Stop worrying
- Accept that you've done your best
- Let go of the situation
- Stop being attached to the outcome

**Questions to Ask Yourself:**
1. What is keeping me up at night?
2. What could I have done better about it?
3. How can I let go of my doubts?

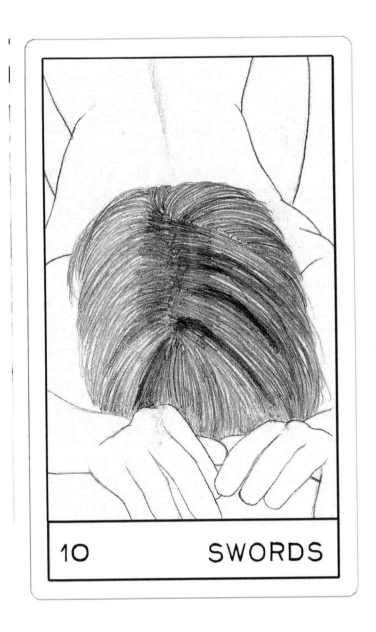

10       SWORDS

# TEN OF SWORDS

Well, ain't that a bitch? After all this fighting and pushing and thinking, you still managed to get the short end of the stick. You're sad and disappointed, and it seems like everything is against you. Get over it. Because it's when you stop fighting that life comes to you and everything flows and fits together. Stop fighting the process and go with the flow. Lay down, dammit!

**Key Phrase:** Stop fighting
**Astrological Correspondence:** Sun in Gemini

**What's Happening:**
- Disaster
- Fighting the flow
- Unexpected results
- Surrendering

**What To Do:**
- Stop fighting the process
- Give in
- If you can't beat them, join them
- Go with the flow

**Questions to Ask Yourself:**
1. What am I fighting against?
2. How did it get to this point?
3. How can I surrender to the situation?
4. How can things improve from this point?

PAGE          SWORDS

# PAGE OF SWORDS

This little hellion will talk a mile a minute, ask you a million questions, and what to know everything from "Why is the sky blue?" to "What is the meaning of life?" He's insanely curious, almost to the point where you just want to tell him to shut the hell up. But he's also crazy smart, and can help you figure out the hairiest of problems. He'll talk you through ideas and help you see the best way to go about making them a reality. Just don't let him hear anything you wouldn't want the world to know  he has a hard time keeping his damn mouth shut.

**Key Phrase:** Seeking the truth
**Astrological Correspondence:** Autumn

**What's Happening:**
- A bold, new idea
- Asking questions
- Being curious
- An inquisitive young person

**What To Do:**
- Pursue a new idea
- Ask questions
- Do some research
- Make a solid plan

**Questions to Ask Yourself:**
1. How am I gaining insight?
2. What message of truth is coming my way?
3. How can I take advantage of this truth?

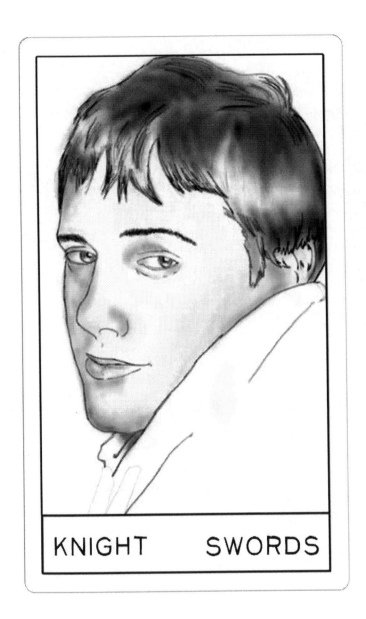

KNIGHT　　　SWORDS

# KNIGHT OF SWORDS

This guy is an asshole. But sometimes, that can be a good thing. Because once he makes up his mind about something, absolutely nothing will stop him from pursuing it. He won't care who he has to run over, and he won't slow down for the idiots in the back. He's passionate and bold, courageous and a bit mysterious  and he's a hit with the ladies. That is, until he puts his foot in his mouth, which he has a tendency to do.

**Key Phrase:** Pursuing your truth
**Astrological Correspondence:** Gemini

**What's Happening:**
- Moving forward alone
- Taking action instead of talking
- Making things happen
- Being a jerk

**What To Do:**
- Less talk, more action
- Go for it, right now!
- Put your ideas into action
- Don't let anything stop you

**Questions to Ask Yourself:**
1. What truth am I pursuing?
2. How am I moving forward in this situation?
3. How can I avoid hurting others as I move forward?

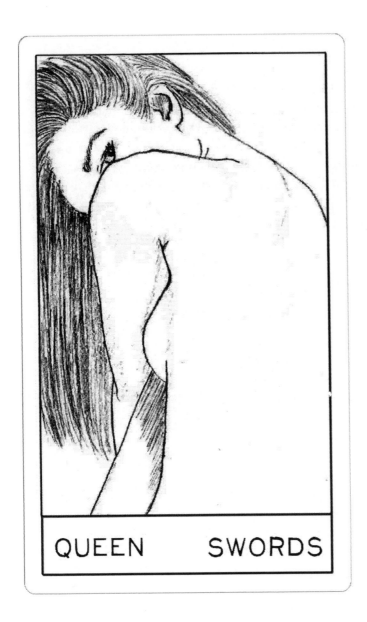

QUEEN      SWORDS

# QUEEN OF SWORDS

This is one sharp lady. She's quick witted, highly intelligent, and dangerously She can joke and debate with the best of them, and she can spot bullshit a mile away. She's had a hard life in the past, so she's street smart and confident in her knowledge. She's a strong, independent lady who can hang with the men, yet still has a soft side. She also has a sharp tongue, and tends to get cynical when she's feeling threatened or vulnerable.

**Key Phrase:** Knowing the truth
**Astrological Correspondence:** Libra

**What's Happening:**
- Having a sharp tongue
- Being quick-witted
- Being perceptive
- Being cynical

**What To Do:**
- Use your intelligence
- Use your sense of humor
- See things for what they are
- Watch out for being mean

**Questions to Ask Yourself:**
1. How can I express my intelligence in this situation?
2. What in my past gives me insight in this situation?
3. How can I cut through to the heart of the situation?
4. How can I be more sensitive in this situation?

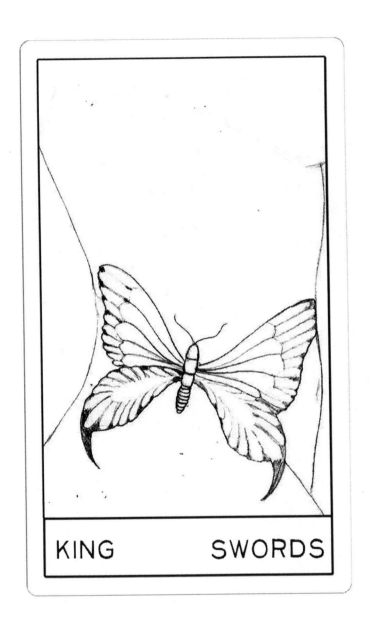

KING        SWORDS

# KING OF SWORDS

This guy has no fucks to give when it comes to emotional bullshit. He's all about the objective, the just and the logical. He's the guy you go to when you want a straightforward analysis of the situation. He'll use his knowledge and mental abilities to tell you exactly what you need to know to make the best decision. Sometimes, though, he can be a real heartless jerk.

**Key Phrase:** Speaking the truth
**Astrological Correspondence:** Aquarius

**What's Happening:**
- Being objective
- Using knowledge to make decisions
- Getting good advice
- Being inflexible

**What To Do:**
- Be unbiased
- Go with what you know
- Be realistic
- Do some research

**Questions to Ask Yourself:**
1. What truth am I sharing?
2. How is my logical mind playing a role?
3. What knowledge am I gaining?
4. How am I using this knowledge?
5. How can I temper my thoughts with compassion?

4        PENTACLES

## PENTACLES

Pentacles are the earthy suit. They represent the body, material wealth, and practical things. They bring up business, education, and things that you can touch and feel.

# ACE OF PENTACLES

This is your golden ticket. This is the opportunity to invest in that brilliant idea that you've been working on. You could even be getting some seed money or practical assistance to help get you started. And you should take advantage of it, because this opportunity could very well turn out to be a gold mine.

**Key Phrase:** New opportunity
**Astrological Correspondence:** Earth Signs

**What's Happening:**
- A new opportunity for money
- Seed money
- A new sexual encounter
- A missed opportunity

**What To Do:**
- Plan for investments
- Invest wisely
- Be open to new chances
- Study and research

**Questions to Ask Yourself:**
1. What's the new opportunity in the situation?
2. What would be the greatest good of this opportunity?
3. How can I create sustainable progress with it?
4. How can I avoid overdoing it?

# TWO OF PENTACLES

You've got your job, your bills, your family  your responsibilities  on one hand, and your personal projects, your entrepreneurial ideas  your dreams  on the other. And somehow, you're keeping things in the air. You're prioritizing, and balancing things quite nicely. Good for you! But be careful... you can't keep juggling forever. Eventually, you're arms are going to get tired. But don't worry  help is on the way.

**Key Phrase:** Flexible multitasking
**Astrological Correspondence:** Jupiter in Capricorn

## What's Happening:
- Juggling responsibilities and fun
- Having fun
- Keeping things in balance
- Dropping the ball

## What To Do:
- Prioritize
- Keep things fun
- Balance work and play
- Keep up the good work

## Questions to Ask Yourself:
1. What situation calls for flexibility?
2. What is in my left hand?
3. What is in my right hand?
4. How can I have more fun in this situation?

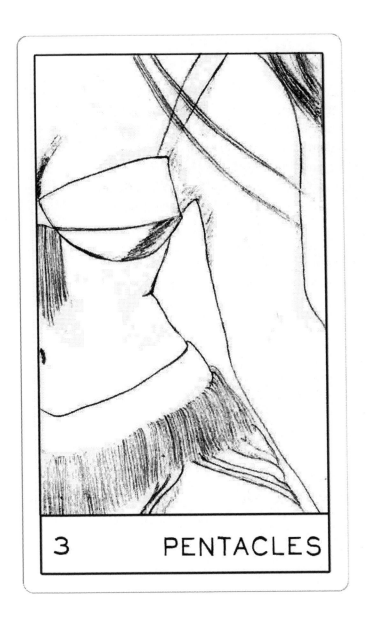

# THREE OF PENTACLES

You've taken your skills and passion, and you've built a reputation for yourself. And people are starting to recognize you and your work. You're enjoying the attention, as you should. In fact, you may be getting commissioned for some work. Someone may be willing to pay you big bucks to do what you do best. Be sure to keep a sense of collaboration in the mix  work with them, even if you don't work for them.

**Key Phrase:** Building your reputation
**Astrological Correspondence:** Mars in Capricorn

**What's Happening:**
- Making a name for yourself
- Creating material goods
- Getting famous
- Not cooperating with others

**What To Do:**
- Communicate your value
- Create physical objects
- Build your reputation
- Work well with others

**Questions to Ask Yourself:**
1. What skills am I being recognized for?
2. How have I built a reputation for myself?
3. How can I use what I've learned to progress?
4. How can I learn from this experience?

4    PENTACLES

# FOUR OF PENTACLES

You are swimming in the dough. You've made a killing with your business, and now you're sitting pretty. You have everything you need. So why do you look so miserable? Well, having everything in the world isn't all that fun when you have no one to share it with. Stop worrying about protecting what you've got, and start letting people into your world.

**Key Phrase:** Holding onto security
**Astrological Correspondence:** Sun in Capricorn

**What's Happening:**
- Stability
- Holding on to what you have
- Being selfish
- Worrying about losing your status

**What To Do:**
- Share what you have
- Make room for new things
- Stop worrying
- Think about what would bring you stability

**Questions to Ask Yourself:**
1. What is the stability that I have created?
2. How is that stability causing me to stagnate in this situation?
3. How can I let go responsibly?
4. How will letting go allow me to build on what I've created?

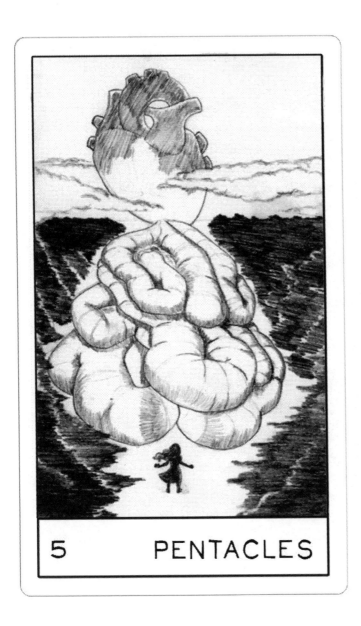

5        PENTACLES

# FIVE OF PENTACLES

Sonuvabitch! Things are tight, and money is looking real funny right now. You're wondering if you're going to be able to pay the bills and things are not looking good. And because of this, you've isolated yourself, thinking that this is something that you have to do alone. But if you'd just look up and reach out to people, you could get the help you need. Stop trying to do it alone.

**Key Phrase:** Ask for help
**Astrological Correspondence:** Mercury in Taurus

**What's Happening:**
- Being broke
- Working towards financial security
- Working alone
- Not asking for help

**What To Do:**
- Look at what you have
- Share the work with others
- Look for ways to make things better
- Ask for help from others

**Questions to Ask Yourself:**
1. What burden am I carrying?
2. Why am I struggling with it?
3. Why do I feel the need to do it alone?
4. Who can I ask for help?

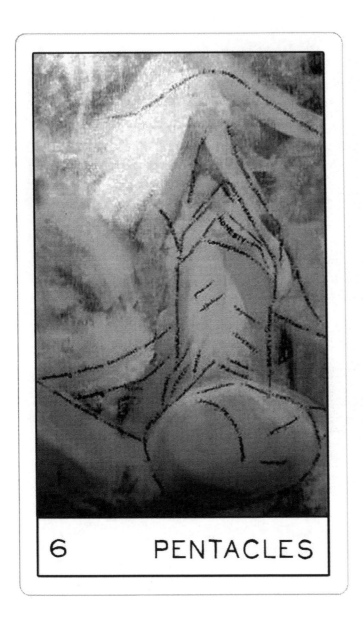

6       PENTACLES

# SIX OF PENTACLES

Well, would you look at that! Somebody was nice enough to actually lend you a hand. You were in need, and they had it to give. And it's not just a handout  the giver benefitted from the gift just as much as the receiver. Don't look a gift horse in the mouth.

**Key Phrase:** Balanced generosity
**Astrological Correspondence:** Moon in Taurus

**What's Happening:**
- Generosity
- Getting help
- Giving what you can
- Overextending yourself

**What To Do:**
- Accept help
- Give what you can
- Change your view about money
- Look for other ways to make money

**Questions to Ask Yourself:**
1. What am I giving?
2. What am I getting in return?
3. What can I give to get more of what I want?

7      PENTACLES

# SEVEN OF PENTACLES

You've put in the work. You've taken time and effort and patience, and you've seen things through. And now you're starting to see results. So do you take the money and run, or do you reflect, reassess and keep working and building something even better? Think about the long term investment and reward, instead of trying to get rich quick.

**Key Phrase:** Pause and assess
**Astrological Correspondence:** Saturn in Taurus

**What's Happening:**
- A long-term project
- Checking your progress
- Seeing results
- Not looking at the long term

**What To Do:**
- Commit to a big project
- Look at what you've done so far
- Decide if you want to keep going
- Look at what can be adjusted

**Questions to Ask Yourself:**
1. What am I working towards?
2. What have I done to get to this point?
3. How are my efforts paying off?
4. How can I make more progress towards my goal?

8    PENTACLES

# EIGHT OF PENTACLES

You've made a name for yourself. You're good at what you do. And that is awesome. You have a steady stream of income, and you are secure for a while. So now would be a good time to delve even deeper into the process. Learn even more, improve your skills. Really focus on the details. It can only make things that much better for you.

**Key Phrase:** Attention to details
**Astrological Correspondence:** Sun in Virgo

**What's Happening:**
- Learning new skills
- Focusing on the process
- Perfecting your skills
- Being a perfectionist

**What To Do:**
- Study and learn
- Pay attention to the details
- Practice
- Stop trying to be perfect

**Questions to Ask Yourself:**
1. What have I learned?
2. How am I putting my knowledge to use?
3. How can I become even more skilled in this situation?

9      PENTACLES

# NINE OF PENTACLES

You've made it. You've worked and scrapped, and asserted yourself, and now you're in the money. You are sitting pretty, and you can afford to indulge and enjoy the luxuries of life. Put on your fancy shoes and nibble on caviar. You've earned it and then some!

**Key Phrase:** Hard-earned luxury
**Astrological Correspondence:** Venus in Virgo

**What's Happening:**
- Comfort and security
- Creating your own prosperity
- Benefiting from your own work
- Not quite at the level of success you'd like

**What To Do:**
- Indulge yourself
- Enjoy what you've created
- Get back to nature
- Keep working towards your goals

**Questions to Ask Yourself:**
1. How did I get to this point in this situation?
2. How can I tame my instincts with discipline?
3. How can I enjoy the fruits of my labor?
4. Am I ready to share what I've earned with others?

10       PENTACLES

# TEN OF PENTACLES

Your successful little venture has now turned into a family business either your family is taking part of the business, or your business is taking care of your family. You should be proud of yourself. You're now able to not only support your family, but you can afford to spend quality time with them as well. Kudos!

**Key Phrase:** Wealthy traditions
**Astrological Correspondence:** Mercury in Virgo

**What's Happening:**
- Long-term stability
- A family business
- An inheritance or scholarship
- A family feud

**What To Do:**
- Consider your long-term success
- Focus on business
- Enjoy the fruits of your labor
- Work through obstacles with your family

**Questions to Ask Yourself:**
1. What am I gaining in this situation?
2. How have I contributed to this situation?
3. What traditions am I becoming a part of now?
4. How can I continue the legacy?

PAGE    PENTACLES

# PAGE OF PENTACLES

This guy usually shows up when you have a new financial opportunity in your life. Maybe you just got a new job, or promotion. Maybe you won the scholarship. Maybe you're just getting a big, fat check. He's all about new ways to make more money. He's really into learning and being book smart, but he could be a little boring sometimes. All in all, he's a good friend to have.

**Key Phrase:** Learning to profit
**Astrological Correspondence:** Winter

**What's Happening:**
- A really stable money-making idea
- Taking studies seriously
- Learning new things
- Being tied to one thing

**What To Do:**
- Pursue business idea
- Pay attention to studies
- Learn something new
- Don't pigeonhole yourself

**Questions to Ask Yourself:**
1. How do I see new opportunities?
2. What opportunity is presenting itself to me?
3. How can I take advantage of this opportunity?

KNIGHT PENTACLES

# KNIGHT OF PENTACLES

This guy is all business, no pleasure. He does nothing but work, work, work all the time. He sets his goals, and he trudges along towards them, taking each obstacle as they come. He's a solid guy, but he tends to miss out on the fun times. He could be great in the sack, but it would be all physical. He's not the lovey-dovey type.

**Key Phrase:** Slow steady progress
**Astrological Correspondence:** Virgo

**What's Happening:**
- Taking your time
- Moving slowly
- Nose to the grindstone
- Being boring

**What To Do:**
- Take your time
- Notice every detail
- Take care of yourself
- Loosen up

**Questions to Ask Yourself:**
1. What am I working towards?
2. How would taking my time benefit me?
3. How can I avoid getting caught up in the details?
4. What is the end result of my labors?

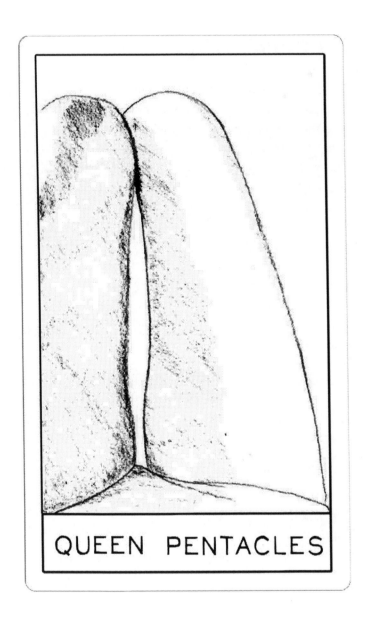

QUEEN PENTACLES

# QUEEN OF PENTACLES

This is the mother hen. She loves everything to do with family and home. She cooks, cleans and decorates the house in order to show her love and success. She organizes the best birthday and dinner parties, and she's always on the PTA or some shit like that. She can be a stubborn broad, and may have some gold- digging tendencies, but all in all, she's like Mother Nature incarnate. She'll feed you, keep you warm, and give you a place to come out of the rain.

**Key Phrase:** Sensible nurturing
**Astrological Correspondence:** Capricorn

**What's Happening:**
- Organizing and planning
- A stay-at-home mom
- Working from home
- Being stubborn and materialistic

**What To Do:**
- Get things organized
- Decorate and adorn
- Take care of yourself
- Learn to be more giving

**Questions to Ask Yourself:**
1. How can I be practical in this situation?
2. How can I be more organized?
3. What am I being called to nurture?
4. How can I show my love in a tangible way?

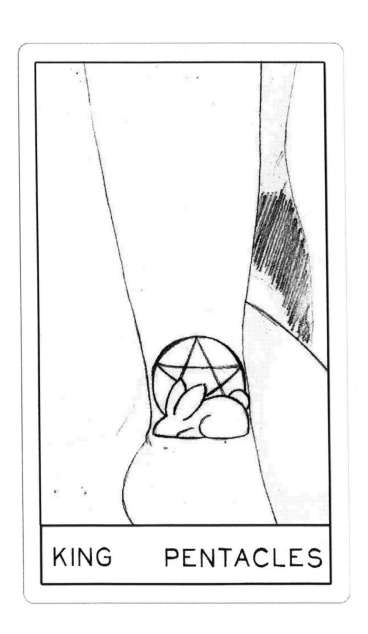

KING     PENTACLES

# KING OF PENTACLES

This is the Donald Trump of the tarot. He's rich, he's successful, and he handles business like no one else. He is smart, savvy and wields power over his kingdom. How did he get there? Through discipline and control he worked his way up from the bottom, and made his own success. And he likes to see that in others, as those are the ones he's most likely to help. Sometimes, he can misuse his power and authority he could be the pervert that looks to help you raise up by putting you on your knees.

**Key Phrase:** Managed resources
**Astrological Correspondence:** Taurus

**What's Happening:**
- Good business deals
- Help from a successful man
- Practical intelligence
- Being blackmailed

**What To Do:**
- Get advice
- Invest wisely
- Work your way to the top
- Accept help from mentors

**Questions to Ask Yourself:**
1. How do I control my resources and assets?
2. How can I use them to help those around me?
3. How do I show my love and affection?
4. How can I be more empathetic to those who aren't so grounded?
5. How can I use my affluence and influence to help others?

# ABOUT THE AUTHOR

Adana Washington is a tarot reader and author of four books on tarot. Her books include **The Sassy Tarot Little White Book**, **Tarot in Real Life: Tarot Meanings for Everyday Life,** and **Tarot Conversations: Tarot Spreads That Create Dialogue**. Two of her books have become Amazon Best Sellers, with copies purchased and read all over the world.

Adana Washington is the creator of the **Kundalini Tarot deck**, and full 78-card tarot deck featuring black and white imagery influenced by kundalini energy. It calls upon corporeal energies to illustrate the symbols and sentiments of tarot. Featuring five years of artwork, the Kundalini Tarot deck provides deeper insights that encourage intuitive interpretations and journeys of self-discovery. Kundalini Tarot is self-published and printed by The Game Crafter.

When she's not working with tarot, Adana enjoys watching anime, learning about witchcraft and metaphysical practices, and baking. She lives in her hometown of Houston, Texas. She can be contacted at adanawtn.com.

Made in the USA
Lexington, KY
07 January 2017